THE GLASS PAINTING BOOK

THE GLASS PAINTING BOOK

JANE DUNSTERVILLE

David & Charles

DEDICATION
This book is dedicated to my husband and my mother
whose creativity and humour are a constant pleasure.

A DAVID & CHARLES BOOK

First published in the UK in 1996
Reprinted in 1997 (three times)
Reprinted in 1998 (three times)
Reprinted in 1999

A catalogue record of this book is available from the British Library

ISBN 0 7153 0428 3

Book design by Jane Forster
Photography by Jonathan Reed

Printed in Great Britain by Butler & Tanner Ltd
for David & Charles
Brunel House Newton Abbot Devon

Contents

Introduction

For several hundreds of years, the only way to paint on glass was to fire-in metallic oxides for details on stained glass windows or else to paint in oils on the back of the glass (the lovely old art of backpainting). However, transparent glass paints became available some years ago, with simpler methods offering the amateur far more scope.

I compare real stained glass with patchwork, and painted glass with appliqué. The colour in real stained glass is a part of the glass itself, and the window is pieced together like patchwork from accurately cut shapes, using an 'H' shaped section of lead, with the joints soldered to create one flat piece. The cost of a stained glass window reflects the skilled craftsmanship that goes into making it, specialist tools, workshop overheads and individual pieces of beautiful glass, some of which will be cut away and wasted of course.

In complete contrast, armed with some glass paints, outline paste and glass jars, a group of children can easily paint jam jar lanterns for an evening around a camp fire. True, it is not the real thing, but many of us would not have the facilities or the time for that. Glass paints have made the great pleasure of working in pure colour more accessible to us all. Many a day-centre has reported the therapeutic effects of colour, while teaching groups have also been excited by the new possibilities.

That was the inspiration for this book. The materials offer such versatility that my own professional projects have been as varied as my clients. For one house I have produced no less than five different bird subjects, taking reference from wildlife books. For many others I have created a formal Victorian-style front door or vestibule in subtle dark tortoiseshell with bottle green, gold and wine red. Only recently I painted a Madonna and Child for a private house, detailed like a chapel, glowing in rich medieval reds and blues, and then sunflowers for a front door. For our own pleasure, my husband John and I have painted fine art pieces featuring myths and legends. Along the way, I have amassed a tremendous body of research and understanding of these new materials. The methods have been fine-tuned by my classes.

I have laid out the methods and variations for you here in their very simplest forms, confident that complete beginners of all abilities can enjoy success. The basics are easily mastered, and the projects are planned to lead you through many additional techniques and build your confidence. The wide variety of designs will inspire you to create an individual piece of your own. So pick up your paint brush and add some colour to your world. The beauty of painted glass offers us a little calm in our busy lives.

JANE DUNSTERVILLE

Materials and equipment

Some of the materials required for this exciting craft, such as the glass, will be very familiar to you, but others less so. It is very reassuring to a beginner, however, to find that some of the methods are similar to those used for other crafts. For instance, those people who are used to watercolours will find that transparent glass paints handle in a similar way, while others compare it to silk painting.

Many also remark that applying the outline is just like working with run-out icing. Those of you who, like me, have never iced a cake, will be pleasantly surprised to know that all mistakes can be removed. You can build up experience by trial and error, confident that the end result will be successful.

We start with a description of all the basic materials, and where to find them. This helpful section includes a Buyer's Guide, which answers all the most common questions and gives tips on working with the materials, when to take care, and how to deal with mistakes and build up confidence. I include simple ideas for convenient work-habits, to prevent paint evaporation and spills.

BUYER'S GUIDE

Glass painting can be set up very economically. Follow these guidelines to track down quality materials, because they are no more expensive than others, and will not go streaky or fade.

As a craft, glass painting does not fit into any category. No established standards cover these materials as yet, so study our Buyer's Guide carefully, and be prepared to ask questions.

THE GLASS
You can use any ordinary glass, nothing special is required. To show the true colours of the paint, clear glass is best. You will find glass at a local glazier, who will cut any shape and size you require and give advice on the thickness. And what about all those jars you have been keeping? Try charity shops too, and pick up plain glass pieces such as bowls, drinking glasses, trinket boxes and plates.

THE OUTLINER
This is acrylic paste, piped around the design straight from the tube, just like icing a cake. It gives a raised black outline, which forms a useful reservoir to hold the paint. Wipe off mistakes with kitchen paper towels while the paste is still wet, or scrape off the outline when it has dried. Outliner dries naturally in about ten minutes, or a hairdryer on a warm setting speeds things up. Always paint over the outline to protect and seal it.

Your will find outline paste in craft shops, and more recently in art shops too. Look for a container like a glue tube. (There is a bigger one, but it will make your thumbs ache!) It is sometimes called contour paste, relief, or misleadingly, liquid lead. There is, in fact, no lead in it at all. You may find it in a number of colours, including black, grey, silver and gold.

ENGINEERING AND FELT TIPPED PENS
These can be used instead of outline paste. The best pen to use is one designed for engineering drawings, using waterproof ink. It will actually write on both glass and plastic, so you may like to try this variation. The finer line of a pen allows for more detailed work, but the disadvantage is that, unlike paste, the pen line will not form a reservoir to separate the colours from each other.

GLASS PAINTS
These are transparent lacquers, of many different types and variable quality, simply applied with a

brush. As with the outliner, mistakes can be wiped off with kitchen paper towels or scraped off when dry. The paint also takes only about ten minutes to dry naturally, but unlike the outliner it must have about two days to harden off properly. Researched in the 1950s, these paints are still considered a very new material. I cover the subject in detail in Your Questions Answered on pages 11–12.

You will find paints in a glazier's or DIY store, which will probably sell single pots of quality paint, or art and craft shops, which will usually have a craft range. Nowadays they are also found in stationers and also in kit form

THE LEAD

This is a strip of real lead with an adhesive backing. It is thin and surprisingly flexible. It will cover sharp edges and allow you to fix an eyelet for hanging. Lead is poisonous, of course, so if you are doing several pieces, wear cotton or polythene gloves. Otherwise, keep food and drink clear and wash your hands after touching it. You will find adhesive lead at a DIY store or a local glazier will help you.

PLASTICS

Plastics are, of course, available in many forms. The following are the main types of plastic used for glass painting.

Rigid plastic sheet, for gardening use or double glazing. It is available from garden centres and from DIY stores. Squares of plastic sheeting may well be available as offcuts. When you buy, ask about the easiest ways of cutting or drilling – for instance, some sheets may need a knife, while others are better sawn. This weight of plastic can be used with a secondary double glazing system to make a panel for your front door or window!

Lightweight film, available from many stationers and art shops. Commercial applications generally include overhead projection and artwork, so it comes in several thicknesses, sometimes on a roll, sometimes in cut sheets of A3 or A4 size. The thickness of film you choose will depend upon the project you have in mind. For example, the window for a greetings card will not need a heavy film as it is supported in the mount. Because film is so much easier to cut than glass (you just use scissors), it works well for mobiles and three dimensional shapes too.

Packaging, ie containers, vacuum packaging, windows in cardboard boxes. You will find pieces everywhere and once you start looking, you won't be able to stop collecting them.

A GOOD BASIC KIT

When looking for a glass painting kit, check that it contains the following:
• Instructions, which must tell you how to clean your brush.
• Outline paste.
• Paints which will mix to make other colours.
• A design to get you started.

It is not strictly necessary to include either a brush or a glass blank because these are readily available, but most kits will do so.

Avoid a kit with a pre-printed design. This will limit your choice, and you will need to buy another kit in order to do more. Master a few very basic techniques with the outline paste, and your choice is limitless!

THINGS TO FIND OUT ABOUT

• Find out what the solvent is for your chosen paints, so that you can clean brushes and mop up spills. Always ask when you buy, because although one pot of paint may look very much like another, each manufacturer uses a different solvent. They can be as different as water, methylated spirits, or white spirits, and there are many others too. The shop where you purchase your materials should be able to explain about their product.

• Choose paints with a reasonable smell. Ask if you may remove the top, and sniff (carefully).

• Check that they will mix.

• Ask if they will fade. Are they intended only for the hobbies market?

• If necessary, ask if there is anyone at the store with specialist knowledge, help and advice.

YOUR QUESTIONS ANSWERED

Here are answers to the most common questions that students ask me about glass painting.

Q What do you use to thin the glass paint?

A The word 'thin' is very misleading: with many other paints, one thinner will clean the brush and make the colours paler. This is not the case with glass paints, so the answer is in two parts.

TO CLEAN THE BRUSH AND ANY SPILLS, you need the solvent which dissolves the paint. As already seen, each make of paint has a different solvent, and you must find out the solvent when you buy your paint.

TO MAKE THE COLOUR PALER, use the clear paint, sometimes called lacquer, of the same manufacture as your other paints. Thinning with the solvent will usually give a streaky finish.

Q Can you mix the colours?

A Not always, so ask when you buy, and be prepared to experiment. Colour-mixing extends the range so much, it is worth finding a make of paints which will intermix. Paints of different manufacture will not normally mix with each other because of the different solvents.

Q Can you wash a painted piece?

A Wipe the paint with a damp, soapy cloth, but dry it straight away. Paints vary greatly, so as a general rule, do not put your painted object under the tap, hot or cold! Never leave it to soak. Always allow plenty of time for the paint to harden off. Never try to wash a piece·where the design is in

outline paste only: it will come off. Always make sure that the outline has been painted over, even if it is with the clear paint, to seal and protect it.

Q Do you need to bake it?

A Most paints are air-drying although some manufacturers recommend baking. You will need to follow their instructions and experiment to see if this does improve durability or lightfastness.

Q Do you lacquer it?

A Most good paints are, in fact, a transparent lacquer, so just by painting the glass, you are forming a lacquered surface. Some manufacturers do suggest a lacquer to finish off, but it is certainly not always the case. They should specify the exact type of lacquer for their paints. The wrong one may cause the finished paint to wrinkle. Contact the manufacturer if you have any difficulties. Again, I recommend first testing it out on a scrap of glass.

Q Will it fade?

A Good quality paints will not fade. Many manufacturers do not guarantee them as lightfast, if displayed in strong sunshine. When buying paints, check that they are suitable for your project.

Q How far will a pot of paint go?

A They really do go a very long way. Some designs use more and some people use more, but both the outliner and the pots of paint would normally do ten or more pieces.

Q Can children do glass painting?

A With individual attention, a child as young as six can produce really good results, but on no account should children play with solvent-based paints – keep them out of sight when not in use.

Q What will it paint on?

A I am often asked if glass paints can be applied to china. They can, of course, because the surfaces are very similar, but many specially formulated paints are already available for china, and these can be fired in, to make them washable.

Any absorbent surface would need a coat of primer to seal it before painting with a lacquer, but you can create some lovely finishes by painting over gold or silver paint. Some of the best effects are discovered by experimenting, with no regard for the rules!

INTRODUCING THE EQUIPMENT

Household equipment will provide most of what you will need to set up glass painting, so once you have found good paints, there is very little further outlay. Gather these basics together every time you start a project, or better still, keep them in a separate box, together with all your paints and brushes, ready to take advantage of those few precious minutes that you have to yourself.

THE BASIC EQUIPMENT
• Clean sheets of old newspaper to cover surfaces for working
• A soft cloth, such as a traditional duster, for cleaning the glass
• A soft paintbrush, select the right size to suit your particular project
• Kitchen paper towels for cleaning the paintbrush and wiping off mistakes when wet
• A craft knife for scraping off mistakes when paints or paste are dry
• A cheap ballpoint pen: use it with the lid on, to burnish a lead edge
• Old scissors to cut lead adhesive
• A reel of masking tape: it will fix your design in place, and you can also use it to support a jar while you apply the paint
• A hairdryer is helpful to speed the drying process
To prepare your design, you will need:
• Tracing paper and a felt-tipped pen, or access to a photocopier to avoid spoiling your book

HANDLING THE MATERIALS

Many of the safe working practices employed when glass painting are common sense. The following procedures will ensure that accidents such as paint spills are kept to a minimum and are easily dealt with, if they do occur.

THE GLASS
Obviously glass has sharp edges, but handled sensibly, it should not be a problem. When cleaning it, lay it flat and never run the cloth along the edges. To pick it up, put your fingers firmly in the centre of the piece, slide it to the edge of the table, and with the other hand, take it between your thumb and first finger, avoiding the edge. Never try to pick up pieces of glass with your finger nails!

ADHESIVE LEAD

Great fun and easy to work with. No particular problems, except that as it is poisonous, you should wear polythene or garden gloves if handling a quantity, and wash your hands afterwards.

OUTLINE PASTE

When you start a new tube of outline paste, open the tube sufficiently for the paste to get out or you might burst the tube. What a mess!

Always keep the kitchen paper towel to hand when using outline paste, and wipe the tip of the nozzle before you start. Whenever you stop, wipe the tip again and put the cap straight on. This simple precaution will save you the unpleasant task of trying to clear the nozzle with a pin when blocked with hardened paste.

Paste on clothes will wash off a garment with water, if treated at once. It is much more difficult after the paste has hardened.

TRANSPARENT GLASS PAINTS

We have already mentioned the importance of finding the right solvent for your paints before you start (see the Buyer's Guide, and Your Questions Answered, pages 8–12). The solvent will clean your brush, as well as any spills on clothes.

Spilt paint may stain a worktop, so good working habits will prevent accidents happening in the first place. Check that you have kitchen paper towel and the right solvent for your paint to hand, and always cover your worksurface with newspapers. If you accidentally knock over a pot of paint, you may be able to pour most of it back in, using the newspaper.

Make sure the room you are working in is well ventilated, it is usually a good idea to open a window to be on the safe side. If you replace the lids on paint pots as you go, you will lose less paint from evaporation and it will be less smelly too!

NIGHTLIGHTS AND CANDLES

A nightlight is perfect for putting inside painted glass containers, such as the jam jars, because the wide, flat base makes it so stable. But do remember never to leave candles alight in a room where there are children or animals unattended by an adult, just in case the candle is knocked over.

THE DESIGN

Whatever your taste and style, our Design Directories will have a design to get you started. Most designs will adapt to fit various shapes and sizes. You may need to use a photocopier to enlarge or reduce the design for your chosen project. It could also be very helpful to make several copies and try out different colour schemes on paper with coloured pencils until you are satisfied.

BASIC
TECHNIQUES

Here you are at the start of a new
and exciting journey: learning to
paint on glass. The projects in this
section introduce you to the most
basic techniques needed to paint
glass – transferring a design,
learning to use outline paste and
handling the transparent glass
paints. With these essential
techniques at your fingertips, you
can develop your repertoire. But do
learn to walk before you think of
running – it pays to consolidate
your skills.

BASIC TECHNIQUES

These tips have been gleaned from watching my classes. Take time to get to grips with materials. Be prepared to experiment and keep it simple.

Before you begin your project, gather together all your equipment, as listed on page 12. Make a habit of working in a tidy way.

THE GLASS

Use clear glass for your projects to bring out the best in your paint colours. Make sure the glass is thoroughly clean before you start. Give jam jars a wash in hot, soapy water and remove labels.

Flat pieces of glass, such as the roundel and glass table top, can be cleaned by putting a little methylated spirit on a soft cloth and wiping over both sides of the glass. Only start working on the glass when the surface is completely dry.

Always adhere to the advice on how to handle glass given on pages 12–13.

USING OUTLINE PASTE

There are several points to watch out for here. The various makes of paste will handle in different ways, and humidity will affect it too. So test it out before you start. Some pastes spread a little, but by adjusting the amount of pressure used to squeeze it out, you can compensate. Warm, dry working conditions are essential.

Different people work in different ways, but by guiding the nozzle tip gently with the hand you write with and squeezing the rolled end with the other, you will be able to use the paste right down to the last drop, and the line will be smooth. Lean well forward so that you can see the design clearly. Bear in mind that once the glass is painted, you will look at the colour, not the line, so if it is a little bit wobbly in places, do not worry.

Always keep paper towels to hand and whenever you stop, wipe the tip of the nozzle with a piece of paper towel and put the cap on straight to avoid getting a blocked nozzle.

REMOVING OUTLINE SMUDGES

Do not worry if you smudge or make a mistake with your outline paste as it is very easily removed. You can simply wipe off the paste if it is still wet, taking great care to do this without removing other parts of the outline.

A second method is to give the paste a quick dry with a hairdryer and use the craft knife to scrape off just the area which is wrong. Then replace the missing line with more outliner and continue with the rest of the outline.

USING TRANSPARENT GLASS PAINTS

Before beginning to paint, make sure that you have the right solvent for cleaning your brush. Then open a window to ventilate the room, and cover your working surface with newspaper.

It can be very difficult to see if the paint is even or not. Apply the paint generously, lifting the glass item now and then to check that the colour is even. It is surprising how different it looks. When flat, the paint seems much more dense and uneven patches do not show. If you check as you go, this can easily be corrected. Glass paints take ten minutes to dry, but allow two days to harden off properly

USING THE DESIGNS

The design directories provide a wide choice of motifs in many styles and subjects. They can be adapted to fit most of the projects in this book.

The best way to use the designs is to photocopy or trace your chosen motif on to a piece of paper. It is possible to trace your motif straight from the book onto flat glass, but you are likely to end up with a very marked book. If you need to alter the size of the design to fit your glass, use the enlarge/reduce key on the photocopier. Take care not to make it too small or complicated for the line thickness of the outline paste.

It is always a very good idea to make a final drawing of the design using a felt-tipped pen of the same thickness as the outline paste you are using. You may then need to simplify the design and it is much better to find this out beforehand. Experiment with different versions until you find the one that works best. These simple guidelines will also help those of you who want to create your own design. Any strong, clear drawing will work on glass or plastic, including those found in children's colouring books, which are perfectly clear.

If you are not sure which colours will work well together, always experiment on the paper design with felt tipped-pens first to build up your colour confidence before committing yourself to your chosen project.

Far Left: Position and secure your design underneath the glass. Supporting your arms firmly on the work surface, touch the tip of the tube right onto the glass. Squeeze the end of the tube gently, while guiding it lightly with your right hand near the nozzle.

Centre: You will be relieved to know that mistakes can be removed! Wipe them off with a tissue while the paste is still wet, or scrape off when dry using a small craft knife as demonstrated here.

Left: Paint generously, so that the paint will flow freely and flatten itself out. Remember to replace the lids of the jars once you have finished to prevent paint evaporation.

Light catcher roundel

Here is a simple project to get you started with outline paste and transparent glass paints. The flat glass surface is easy to work and of a manageable size, allowing you to cover the surface with the pretty design shown here.

You can follow the colour scheme in the picture or choose your own, perhaps using your favourite colours. It is a good idea to keep the number of colours you use to a minimum to begin with, until you get used to applying and changing the paint colours. Hang your roundel in a window and see how the colours glow in the light. There are more motifs in the Design Directory on pages 20–23.

TECHNIQUE FOCUS

Tracing a design, using outline paste, transparent glass paints and adhesive lead strip

MATERIALS

6in (150mm) – diameter glass roundel
Methylated spirit
Adhesive lead strip
Thin wire
Pliers
Solder
Your design
Outline paste
Transparent glass paints
The right solvent for the paints you have chosen
Decorative ribbon (optional)
Basic equipment as listed on page 12

1 Lay the glass flat and clean it on both sides with a little methylated spirit on the soft cloth. Lay the adhesive strip on your work surface, with the waxy backing upwards. Smooth it out using the ballpoint pen, and then peel off the backing to reveal the adhesive.

2 Stand the roundel on its edge on the lead strip and roll it along the middle of the strip. If you go off-centre, roll back and reposition.

3 As you roll the glass along, pinch the lead around onto it with your thumb and forefinger. Continue right around the edge of the glass. Trim the excess lead with old scissors.

4 Now make the wire loop for hanging the roundel by folding the thin wire over the handle of the paintbrush. Take hold of the two ends with pliers and turn the brush once or twice. Cut the legs to about ½in (12mm) long and open out. Slip the legs under the folded lead edge, taking care to push them in well.

5 Lay the roundel flat and burnish the lead down with the lid of the ballpoint pen. Press flat any lumps before smoothing and burnishing firmly, especially around the wire loop. For added security, solder the join. Clean the glass again.

6 Prepare your design as described on page 17. Place the design face up and position the glass on top of it. Tape the design in place with masking tape.

8 Paint generously using the soft paintbrush with the transparent paints. Clean the brush with the solvent and paper towels when changing colours. Lift the glass off the table now and then to check that the colour is even. Paints will dry in about ten minutes, and again a hair dryer will help, but allow two days for the paints to harden properly.

7 Use the outline paste to trace the design. Mistakes can be wiped off with paper towels. Leave the outline paste for about ten minutes to dry naturally or use a hair dryer to speed up the drying time. Then carefully remove the design from the back of the glass.

9 A decorative ribbon tied in a bow at the top of the roundel makes a pretty finishing touch. If your window has a wooden frame, you may like to use a screw-in hook and hang your roundel on nylon fishing line. An adhesive pad will secure a hook to a plastic or metal frame.

Design directory

Circular table-top

This is an enchanting, full size project for the sitting room or bedroom. Pretty and practical, it is also quite straightforward to do, simply applying the methods used in the roundel to a larger piece of glass.

For your design, choose between a circlet of flower blossoms or a trail of classic ivy provided in the Design Directory on pages 26–27. These timeless designs will add to any decorative scheme because they are so peaceful and easy to live with. Or how about painting a dragon or bird of paradise, in exotic colours?

When buying the glass, ask your glazier to advise you on a safe thickness for the size of your table. Consider any special circumstances in your home (like children who may pull the tablecloth), and ask if the glass will need to be toughened. Make sure you ask for the edges to be rubbed down, making it much safer and easier to handle. The 'transparent bumps' listed below act as supports for the glass, raising it slightly off the table and can also be purchased from a glazier.

TECHNIQUE FOCUS
Working on a large project

MATERIALS
Sheet of paper (large enough for the pattern)
Circular side-table
Glass to fit (20in [50cm]-diameter circle used here)
Your design
Glue stick
Outline paste
Transparent glass paints
The right solvent for the paints
you have chosen
Transparent adhesive bumps
Basic equipment as listed on page 12

1 Use the paper towel to clean the glass. To prepare your design, place the sheet of paper flat with the glass table-top on it. Draw around it with the marker pen and then cut out the circle with the scissors. Fold the paper circle in half and mark the crease clearly with the pencil. Fold again to mark the quarters in the same way.

2 Photocopy your chosen design from the Design Directory on pages 26–27, making four copies of the design. Cut out the four design motifs and lay them out, each within a section, to form a circle. Decide on any modifications you wish to make, pulling the design motifs nearer to the edge, or in towards the centre. For a different size table-top, it may be necessary to add or remove a design motif. When satisfied, stick all the motifs in place with the glue stick.

3 Place the design face up and position the glass on top of it. Tape the design in place with masking tape.

4 Use the outline paste to trace the design. Mistakes can be wiped off with a paper towel. Leave the outline paste for about ten minutes to dry naturally or use a hair dryer to speed up the drying time. Then carefully remove the design from the back of the glass.

5 Paint generously using the soft paintbrush with the transparent paints. Clean the brush with the solvent and paper towels when changing colours. Lift the glass off the table now and then to check that the colour is even. Like the outliner, paints will dry in about ten minutes, and again a hair dryer will help, but do allow two days for the paints to harden off properly.

6 Peel the adhesive bumps off their backing, one at a time, and position them discreetly between the leaves so that the glass will be well supported. Place a light coloured cloth on the table. Turn the glass over, so that the design is face downwards, and position the glass table-top over the cloth. The bumps will lift the glass off the cloth, so that it is not spoilt, and the top surface will be very easy to clean.

Design directory

Note that the two central motifs join together, as indicated in the small diagram.

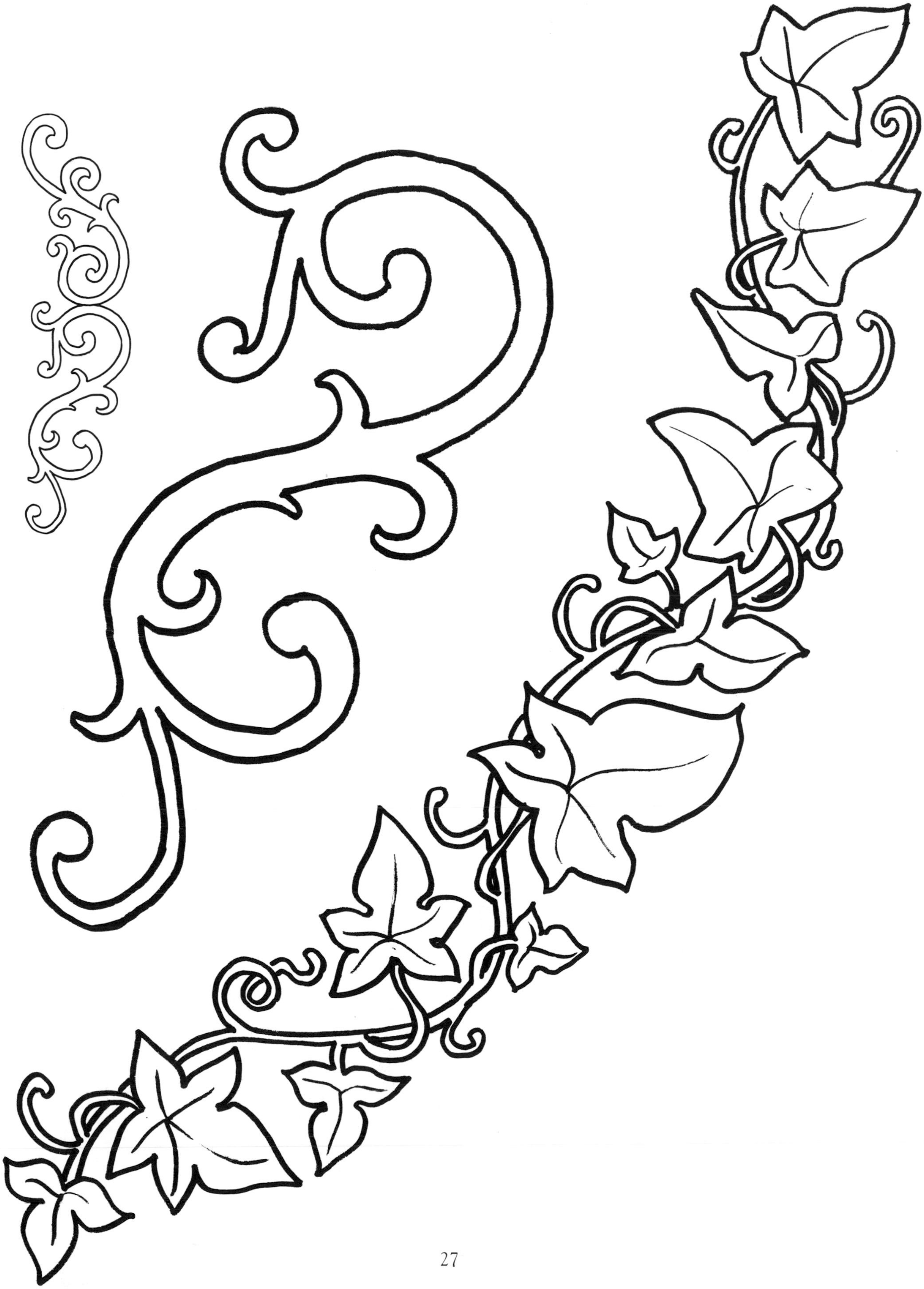

Garden lanterns

 The humble jam jar takes on a new dimension when it is transformed into a stunning lantern for a summer barbecue, or a dreamy nightlight for a child's bedroom.

The supply of jars is abundant, and free, which means that they are perfect for practising a new technique, painting on a vertical, curved surface. The simple but effective designs featured here are all drawn freehand and can be used on a jar of any shape or size. Use them as a starting point, but then branch out on your own and have fun making up your own patterns and colour schemes. You may want to sketch out your pattern on a piece of paper first of all before drawing it with outline paste on the side of the jar. Always use clear glass jars as this brings out the true colours of the paints to best advantage. Before starting, thoroughly wash and dry your jars in hot, soapy water, and then check that the nightlight comfortably fits inside if you intend the jar to be a lantern.

TECHNIQUE FOCUS
Painting freehand patterns on a vertical
curved surface

MATERIALS
Jam jars
Large tape-reel
Freehand pattern
Outline paste
Transparent glass paints
The right solvent for the paints you have chosen
Nightlights
Basic equipment as listed on page 12

1 Thoroughly wash the jam jar in hot, soapy
water and dry. Then, to support the jar while
you are working, lean it inside the tape reel.

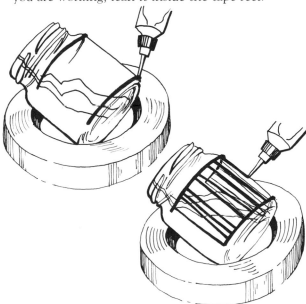

2 With the outline paste, draw a border around
the top and bottom of the jam jar as far as
you can reach without smudging it.

3 Now fill the area between the top and bottom borders with vertical lines to make a
panel. Don't worry if the lines are uneven or
crooked; it all adds to the character of your work,
making it more like stained glass. To complete
the panel, draw on lots of short, horizontal lines.

4 Use the hairdryer to dry the paste. When it is
hard enough to rest in the tape reel without
smudging the first half, turn the jar around and
finish drawing lines on the rest of the glass in the
same way. Dry as before.

5 To paint the jar, pick it up by bunching your
fingers in the top, so that you can easily turn
it. Start with one colour, for example yellow, a
typical lantern colour, and paint at random right
the way around.

6 Choose another colour and again, paint ran-
domly; then pick a third, and a fourth colour,
and as the spaces fill up, you complete the
stained-glass effect.

7 Finish by choosing a colour for the areas outside the panels at the top and bottom and
brush it on lightly all around.

VARIATIONS

The basic approach for the patchwork pattern also
applies to the two other patterns featured on the
left, one using wavy lines, the other zigzag. Try
doing these patterns and then make up some of
your own. You could do something more geomet-
ric, like the colourful jar below.

Picture lanterns

Once you have mastered painting freehand on a jar as described on the previous two pages, try using a trace-off motif. Tracing a motif onto a curved surface is a little more difficult, but with a bit of practice, you will soon master the technique.

The design has to be carefully positioned inside the jar so that all of the lines are visible. To ensure an accurate tracing of your pattern, push some crumpled sheets of newspaper inside the glass to hold the design directly against it as you work. Choose your design from the wealth of motifs given on pages 32–3, or you might prefer to look at some of the other Design Directories in the book to see if there is another motif which is right for your jar. Alternatively, you could decide to create your own design taking your inspiration from nature or ideas gleaned from visits to galleries.

TECHNIQUE FOCUS
Using a trace-off design on a curved surface

MATERIALS
Jam jars
Your design
Outline paste
Transparent glass paints
The right solvent for the paints you have chosen
Nightlights

Basic equipment as listed on page 12

Enjoy experimenting with designs and allow the shape of the jar to suggest ideas. The simple tree design is outlined on all four sides of this jar, with colours carefully selected to evoke the four seasons. Tiny dots of pure white, without outliner, are used for the snow.

1 Wash the jam jar in hot, soapy water and dry. Prepare your design, cut it out carefully and fix it to the inside of the jar, facing outwards, using two small pieces of masking tape. If necessary, use scissors to reach down inside the jar and manipulate the design. If the picture does not lie neatly against the glass, push some crumpled newspaper in behind it, so that you will get a good, clear image.

2 Now rest the jar in the tape reel at a comfortable angle for working and use the outline paste to trace the design onto the glass. Mistakes can be wiped off with paper towels.

3 When you are happy with it, dry the outline with the hairdryer and remove the paper from inside the jar, with the help of the scissors.

4 To paint the jar, pick it up by bunching your fingers in the top so that you can easily turn it. Paint generously, using the soft paintbrush with the transparent paints. Use the kitchen paper and solvent to clean the brush in between mixing colours. Allow the paint to harden off for at least two days.

Design directory

Carriage lantern

A warm welcome awaits you with this glowing lantern to light your way home. You may like to decorate a carriage lantern either to light a porch by the front door or to make a colourful focal point for the garden on a summer evening.

A variety of light fittings and candle holders is available in a lantern style, and most of them have removable glass panes. Good quality paints will not be affected by heat from either a candle or a light bulb. Trace your chosen design from the Design Directory on pages 36–37 using outline paste, as for the roundel. Or if you are feeling more adventurous, create freehand patterns as described on pages 28–29 for the Garden Lanterns.

TECHNIQUE FOCUS

Consolidating your outlining and painting skills

MATERIALS

Lantern

Your design

Outline paste

Transparent glass paints

The right solvent for the paints you have chosen

Basic equipment as listed on page 12

1 Before removing the glass from the frame, use paper towels to clean it. Remove the glass panes from the frame, taking great care to avoid the sharp edges. If the glass is too stiff to remove easily from the fitting, use masking tape to help you. Take a length of tape, stick it to the top edge of the glass, and use it to pull the glass carefully upwards, out of the frame.

2 Clean off any finger marks left from handling the glass. When choosing and positioning your design, remember to leave a border around the edge, to clear the metal tags which hold the glass panes in place. If you paint right to the edge, your work may be spoilt by the fitting itself, when replacing the glass.

3 Prepare your design as described on page 17. Then place it face up and position the glass on top of it. Neatly tape the design in place with masking tape.

4 Use the outline paste to trace the design. Mistakes can be wiped off with paper towels. Leave the outline paste for about ten minutes to dry naturally or use a hair dryer to speed up the drying time. Then carefully remove the design from the back of the glass.

5 Paint generously using the soft paintbrush with the transparent paints. Clean the brush with the solvent and paper towels when changing colours. Lift the glass off the table now and then to check that the colour is even. Like the outliner, paints will dry in about ten minutes, and again a hair dryer will help, but do allow two days for the paints to harden off properly.

6 Replace the glass panes in the lantern fitting. If it is for a permanent external fitting, the painted side can be turned inwards to assist weather-proofing.

Design directory

Peacock cupboard door

I am asked time and again about painting doors and windows. So here is a basic method for full-sized vertical projects. I always suggest that it is easier to experiment on a small project, before tackling the front door!

A kitchen or bathroom cabinet is just the right size for you to try out ideas and find a good method suitable for the project. Usually the door can be removed from such a cupboard or cabinet. If this is possible, you will find it much easier to lay the project flat, but with this project there is detailed help given for painting on a vertical surface.

Whichever method you choose, aim to keep the painted glass surface on the inside of the cupboard. This will not only make it easier to clean, but will also protect it from steam, grease and everyday wear and tear.

TECHNIQUE FOCUS

Painting on a vertical surface

MATERIALS

Cupboard or cabinet

Your design

Outline paste

Transparent glass paints

The right solvent for the paints you have chosen

Basic equipment as listed on page 12

1 Use paper towels to clean the glass. Prepare your design as described on page 17. Then, if it is possible to lay the door flat, place the design face up and position the glass on top of it. Tape the design in place with masking tape. If this is not possible, open the cupboard door, and decide on which side the surface will be painted. The painted surface should be inside the cupboard, so position the design on the outside of the glass, facing into the cupboard.

2 Working on the inside of the glass, use the outline paste to trace the design. Mistakes can be wiped off with paper towels. Leave the outline paste for about ten minutes to dry naturally or use a hair dryer to speed up the drying time. Remove the design from the back of the glass.

3 Paint generously, using the soft paintbrush with the transparent paints. Clean the brush with solvent and paper towels between colours.

4 If painting vertically, load the brush well with paint, start at the top of a section, and when you reach the bottom, wipe excess paint off your brush back into the pot. Finish by brushing lightly downwards over that area, and allow the paint to flatten out. With the brush, wipe out any runs that may form in the paint. To speed up the process, use a hair dryer to dry a section at a time.

5 If painting flat, lift the glass off the table now and then to check that the colour is even. The paints will dry in about ten minutes, and again a hair dryer will help, but allow two days for the paints to harden off properly.

6 Doors can be rehung within a day, but avoid getting finger marks in the painted areas, as the paint will remain 'tender' for a further day or two. If working vertically, you will be less able to protect the surface so that it can harden off. So over the next two days take care to protect it from inquisitive fingers.

Design directory

Globe lightshade

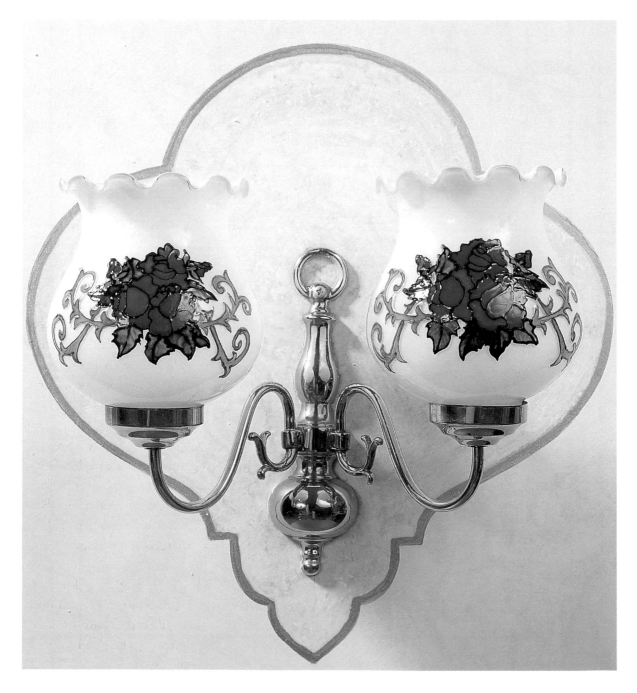

A completely round glass object makes it a little more tricky to position a motif properly against the glass surface, but here you will learn how to deal with this rather awkwardly-curved shape.

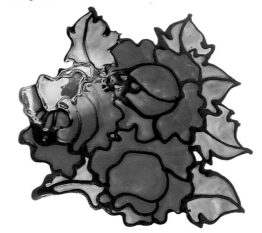

Any project with a double curvature, such as this globe light shade designed for a wallmounted light or round, glass bowl, will need tucks cut into the design to make it lie flat against the glass. This must be taken into consideration when you are choosing and arranging the design, as some of it may get lost in the tucks. You may find it easier to use a single large motif, or to repeat a simple small motif. Try out your design carefully for fit before starting.

Test ways of placing the item at a good angle to work with, so that it will not move, and it is also easy to handle.

TECHNIQUE FOCUS
Dealing with a double curvature

MATERIALS
Globe lightshade
Your design
Outline paste
Transparent glass paints
The right solvent for the paints you have chosen
Basic equipment as listed on page 12

1 Wash the lightshade in hot, soapy water and dry. Prepare your design. Remember to cut small tucks in the paper pattern so that it lies against the glass. Position it inside the lightshade, facing outwards exactly as you did for Garden Lanterns on pages 28–29. Tape it in place.

2 With the lightshade resting comfortably, use the outline paste to trace the design. Leave the paste to dry naturally or use a hairdryer to speed up the drying process. Remove the design from inside the project.

3 Secure the lightshade comfortably for painting. Paint generously, cleaning the brush with the solvent and paper towel in between changing colours. Like the outliner, paints will dry in about ten minutes, and again a hairdryer will help, but do allow two days to harden off properly.

Try this more difficult technique on the clear bowl first, then progress to the opaque glass light fitting. You will need to place a light behind the opaque glass so that the pattern can be clearly seen through the glass while you trace and paint the design.

Design directory

COLOUR
SENSE

Now that you are familiar with the basic
ways in which glass paints can be used, it
is time to experiment with colour. Here
we find out how to go beyond using
colours straight from the bottle into how
to mix colours to increase your colour
range, and achieve just the right colour
for the project in hand. We also cover
how to use white, the most difficult of
glass paint colours.

COLOUR SENSE

The essence of this section is the excitement you feel when first learning how to mix paint colours. This will extend your colour range dramatically.

THE PALETTE

Before starting work, make a palette on which you can mix the paints. For small quantities of paint, clean a small foil container from, say, a fruit pie and use it for mixing. If you prefer to mix against a white background, wrap several layers of plastic wrap over an old white saucer or plate. When mixing colours, remember that paints will evaporate, so this is not the time to go and answer the telephone. Larger quantities of your favourite colours can be mixed in a screw top jar.

MIXING COLOURS

Always start with the lightest colour, and add a little at a time, stirring well, or you can make gallons of paint before you reach the right colour!

USING WHITE: BEWARE!

White really is a rogue colour, because it is not transparent. To imagine the effect, think of white gloss paint on a window: it blocks out the light. It takes some skill to make white look pretty, mixing just a few drops with any colour, to achieve a soft, etched look, which catches the light. To be able to see what you are doing as you paint, you need a dark background.

For a roundel or any piece that will be seen against daylight, use a mixture of mainly clear glass paint with just a little white. If you find it is just looking heavy and treacly, paint quickly all over the area with clear paint, which will soften and wet it so that it flows again. Lift the roundel off the work surface often, to see how the paint looks.

For a jam jar or any piece which will be seen against a dark background, use white straight from the pot, but do bear in mind that white paint over a black outline paste will spoil it. There is no perfect method, because the white paint is opaque, unlike all the other glass paints.

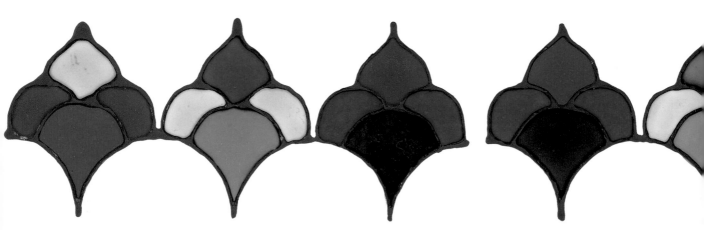

Primary colours

These cannot be made by mixing, so they must be purchased. They are red, yellow and blue.

Mixing secondary colours (above palette)

The three secondary colours are orange, green and purple and are made by mixing two primary colours:
ORANGE: start with yellow, add a little red, stir well.

GREEN: start with yellow, add a little blue, stir well.
PURPLE: start with red, add a little blue, stir well.

Mixing tertiary colours (centre palette)

Mix together any three colours to make a tertiary colour, for example:
BROWN: use yellow and red to make orange, add blue, and stir well.

Methods for using white

• It is not too difficult to paint inside a jar, with a long-handled brush. But if you do not paint over the outline, it remains unprotected against washing later on. Paint over the outline with clear paint to seal it.
• Paint on the outside as usual, but avoid the black outline, and then paint that with clear paint to protect it.
• Paint white on the outside, as usual, over the black outline to protect it. When it is dry, use a black permanent marker pen to blacken the outline again. This process is rather tedious, but quite effective. Allow the paint to harden off for a day.

Colour mixing with white

If you are to avoid a range of yogurt-like colours, add only a drop of white at a time. Study the photograph of the moon lightcatcher on page 99, for example. In bright sunlight, all the colours glow, but against a dark background, the yellow alone shines out. The yellow has a drop of white added to it. This is a very interesting variation, and something you will probably want to experiment with.

CHOOSING COLOURS

When painting nature, you will find that a simple process of elimination works well for choosing a colour scheme. If you paint leaves green, flower centres yellow, and anything else identifiable in the right colours, it is a foregone conclusion.

You may only have to decide on a colour for the outside edge, in which case take care not to compete with the main design. Paint this in a matching or contrasting colour.

Choosing colours for a formal design is not so easy as there is no starting point. In this case it is especially helpful to try different colourways on copies of the paper design. Look through magazines to find a colour group which appeals to you. Then try the same colour group in different ways to see what you like the best.

How much to leave clear

Again, this is a matter of personal taste, but try to achieve a balance between the coloured and the clear areas, so that the eye has somewhere to rest.

LIME GREEN: *use yellow and blue to make green, add yellow, and stir well.*
MAGENTA: *use red and blue to make purple, add red, and stir well.*

Mixing darker colours (right-hand palette)
To create a moodier effect, add brown, blue or black to your original mix.

Mixing lighter colours
Surprisingly, avoid white. Start with clear glass paint and add the colour you wish to make paler a few drops at a time. Stir well. For skin colour: start with clear and add a little brown, stir well. Peach: start with clear, add a little brown and a little red, stir well. Pink: start with clear, add a little magenta and a little red, stir well.

Rainbow jar

This pretty project will allow you to try out several of your newly acquired techniques and also introduces using white glass paint, a most particular and exciting effect, the pure opaque white contrasting with the clear rainbow colours.

This lovely rainbow design uses white paint straight from the pot and clearly illustrates the effect this colour has on glass. The opaque effect works well in this design, but think carefully about its effect before incorporating it into other designs. The motifs given in the Design Directory on the pages that follow can all use unmixed white paint.

TECHNIQUE FOCUS
Using white glass paint

MATERIAL
Your design
Large plain jar
Outline paste
Transparent glass paints
Palette
The right solvent for the paints you have chosen
Black permanent marker pen (optional)
Nightlight candle
Basic equipment as listed on page 12

1 Prepare your design, cut it out carefully and fix it to the inside of the jar, facing outwards, using two little pieces of masking tape. Use scissors to reach down inside the jar to help manipulate the design. However, if the picture does not lie perfectly flat against the glass, push some crumpled newspaper in behind it, so that you will get a good clear image.

3 Paint generously, using the soft paintbrush with the transparent paints. If you are using the rainbow design, use the photograph opposite as a colour guide, and mix the required colours according to the advice on page 50. Use the paper towels and solvent to clean the brush in between mixing colours.

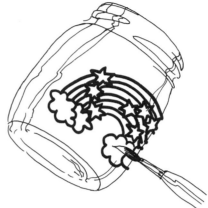

4 When painting the clouds white, you will find that white paint can spoil the black outline. There is no perfect method because the white paint is opaque, unlike all the other glass paints, so any solution can only be a compromise. Choose from one of the methods outlined on pages 50–51 Allow the paint to harden off for at least a whole day.

5 Stand the finished jar on a window ledge and see the differences between the transparent colours and the opaque white. For safety's sake, move it away from the window to keep it clear of curtains, and light a nightlight candle. Lower the lighted candle into the jar using a long pair of scissors or kitchen tongs, and look again at the way the light affects the colours, so that you can judge for yourself the effect you will achieve on other projects of your own.

2 Now rest the jar in the tape reel at a comfortable angle for working and use the outline paste to trace the design onto the glass, piping the paste directly from the tube. Mistakes can be wiped off with paper towels. Leave the outline paste for about ten minutes to dry naturally or use a hair dryer to speed up the drying time. Carefully remove the design with the help of the scissors.

Design directory

Decorative paperweight

A stand-up paperweight frames the subject of these unusual portraits, giving an opportunity to mix white for dramatic effects. Here white is mixed with clear for a translucent, etched look, and with other colours to achieve some subtle shades.

We will be painting on the back of the glass, so this time there is no problem with spoiling the outline. This is a similar method to the popular Victorian method of 'back-painting' onto the reverse side of glass, but they used opaque paints, usually oils.

Trace the motifs given here or make a paperweight featuring your own pet . Take a photograph of your pet against a light background, then make a tracing of its outline. Use a photocopier to reduce or enlarge the tracing to the right size for your paperweight.

TECHNIQUE FOCUS
Mixing white paint with clear

MATERIAL
Your design
Round, stand-up paperweight
Outline paste
Transparent glass paints (including clear and white)
Palette
The right solvent for the paints you have chosen
Basic equipment as listed on page 12

1 Prepare your drawing, as described above. The picture will be positioned on the back of the glass, so your design is reversed. Writing should be reversed on the original drawing, which makes it the right way round on the finished work.

2 Place the paperweight face down with the base towards you, and clean the recessed back thoroughly with a paper towel. Take the prepared drawing and place it face up, with the paperweight on top, face down. Check that the drawing is level with the base, so that your design is not leaning over!

3 The thick glass will make it difficult to focus on the picture, so close one eye as you use the outline paste to trace the outline. Care is needed on a small subject such as this, so take time to adjust the flow of the paste. Be prepared, also, to dry the paste and trim carefully with the craft knife to create exactly the right expression on your pet's face. Leave the outline paste for about ten minutes to dry naturally or use a hair dryer to speed up the drying time. Remove the design from the back of the glass.

4 With the paintbrush, place some clear paint on the palette, and add a drop of white. Mix well, checking that you have enough paint for the area to be painted. Paint the white parts of the picture. Hold the paperweight over a dark background, so that any uneven patches show. Adjust the colour until it is even. Finish all of the white parts in the same way. As you are painting on the back, the outline will not be affected.

5 Any other parts of the design painted with transparent colours will 'disappear' in comparison with the white, so mix a little white with all the other colours to balance the picture. With the brush, place some clear glass paint on the palette, and a drop of white as before. Squeeze the

brush into a piece of paper towel and take a drop of the next colour required, blending all three on the palette. Continue, painting a colour at a time. When changing colours, clean the brush with a paper towel and the solvent.

6 When the picture is finished, pay particular attention to removing all the white paint from the brush with the solvent. White is very persistent, and if it is not scrupulously cleaned out, it will contaminate other colours.

Photograph frames

Simplicity itself, painting a photograph frame is a delightful way to add a personal finishing touch to a treasured memory or family pictures. Amongst the three delightful approaches here and overleaf you will find a motif to please all ages.

Use these ideas for a display of photographs, or make a present to mark a special occasion. They make the ideal opportunity for experimenting with mixing colours on your palette.

TECHNIQUE FOCUS

Using the three colour-groups: primary, secondary and tertiary

ONCE UPON A TIME

The easiest design, bound to fit most frames, is one that embellishes just a corner, or perhaps top and bottom. Use this dear little design of a teddy bear and some ABC building blocks for a new baby. For a lovely surprise, match the frame to the colours that the real nursery will be. Make the design larger or smaller to choice, and perhaps add more building blocks to make a border all around.

MATERIALS

Photograph frame with mount (any shape or size)
Felt-tipped marker pen
Your design
Outline paste
Transparent glass paints
Palette
The right solvent for the paints you have chosen
Basic equipment as listed on page 12

1 With the frame still assembled as purchased, clean the glass carefully with a damp cloth and dry. Then, using the felt-tipped marker pen,

trace the shape of the mount onto the glass, so that when positioning your design, you can see which area to leave clear for the photograph. Remove the glass from the mount and frame and set them aside well out of the way.

2 Prepare your design, then place it face up and position the glass on top of it. Keep the design within the shape of the mount, making sure that the photograph will not be obscured. Tape the design in place with masking tape, and then clean the felt-tipped line using paper towels.

3 Lightly remove any finger marks again, and trace the design with outline paste. Mistakes can be wiped off with paper towels. Leave the outline paste for about ten minutes to dry naturally or use a hair dryer to speed up the drying time.

4 Remove the design from the back of the glass. You could decide now whether to be more ambitious, if space allows, and add other building blocks around the outside. See how it all looks with the photograph, and try out some ideas. If in doubt, leave well alone.

5 Start by painting the teddy bear yellow, and then the rest of the design can be painted the colours of your choice, so just have fun! If you like strong primaries, use red, yellow and blue paints straight from the pots, as they are. But if pastels are your choice and you fancy a bit of colour mixing, take a brushful of clear glass paint and blend it on the palette with other colours to make softer shades. Use the solvent and paper towels to clean the brush when changing colours. Paint generously, so that brush marks will blend and disappear.

6 Allow the paint to harden off for two days. When you reassemble the frame, mount and photograph, take care to avoid fingerprints on painted surfaces. This simple method will work well on any photograph or picture, so it could give you ideas for mounting a piece of cross stitch or quilling too.

Left: Simple nursery motifs in pure primaries – red, yellow and blue – capture the simple delight of a child. This would make an ideal gift for proud grandparents or even a special aunt.

Right: Echoes of ethnic patterns in the more moody, secondary colours – orange, green and purple – reflect those turbulent teenage years.

ROUND THE WORLD

Elements of world art unite for a border design with options for individual choice. Experiment with mixing secondary colours and exciting decorative techniques.

MATERIALS

Your border motifs
A4 Clip frame
Glue stick
Outline paste
Transparent glass paints
Palette
The right solvent for the paints you have chosen
Basic equipment as listed on page 12

1 The basic layout sheet given in the Design Directory on pages 62–65 shows a quarter of the A4 size border. With the A4 tracing paper, make a full size layout sheet. Photocopy or trace your preferred design motifs, and cut them out with the scissors. Then use the layout sheet to position the motifs and the photograph until you are satisfied. Glue the motifs into their final positions and remove the photograph

2 Remove the glass from the clip frame and put the backing out of the way, too. Clean the glass with the cloth. Place the prepared design face up and position the glass on top of it. Tape the design in place with masking tape.

3 Use the outline paste to trace the design. Mistakes can be wiped off with paper towels. Leave the outline paste for about ten minutes to dry naturally or use a hair dryer to speed up the drying time. Remove the design.

4 Use the coloured pencils to try out some colour schemes on the paper pattern. The secondary colours, orange, green and purple, appeal to the teens and young-adult age-group. Pick out the colours in the picture or photograph, or try a complete contrast.

5 When you are happy with the result, paint the glass, starting again at the centre, using the paintbrushes and transparent glass paints. Decide which brush to use, according to whether you are painting a detail or filling a large area. Use the solvent and paper towels to clean the brush when changing colours. Blend and mix colours, using a brushful or just a drop of colour, as required.

6 Allow the finished frame to harden off for two days. Glue the photograph into position on the backing and reassemble the frame.

NOW, WHEN I WAS A GIRL

An Edwardian-style design, reminiscent of rich tortoiseshell and marble finishes, cherishes the sepia print of a family portrait. In choosing the colours for this more formal theme, take care not to overshadow the photo itself: it may be appropriate to keep the scheme quite soft, mixing all the colours with clear paint. Perhaps a subtle group of amber and brown is called for: a true tertiary group.

MATERIALS
Photograph frame with a mount
Outline paste
Your design
Coloured pencils (optional)
Transparent glass paints
Palette
The right solvent for the paints you have chosen
Basic equipment as listed on page 12

1 With the frame still assembled as purchased, clean the glass carefully with the damp cloth and then leave to dry.

2 Using the outline paste, trace the shape of the mount onto the glass. Make this quite a thick line, so that it is easy to reposition when finished. The outline will dry in ten minutes, but you can speed it up with a hair dryer. Mistakes can be wiped off with paper towels or scraped away with the craft knife. Remove the mount and frame from the glass, and set aside well out of the way.

3 Prepare your design, then place it face up and position the glass on top of it. Tape the design in place with masking tape.

4 Lightly remove any finger marks again, and trace the design with more outline paste. Allow the finished outline to dry as before and take off the paper pattern.

The gentle curves of this flowing design are reminiscent of the Art Nouveau style. They have been painted in elegant tertiaries. Subtle browns and greys – natural colours of the earth and stone – blend for a mature, sophisticated image that complements the old photograph.

5 A monochrome colour group needs careful planning if it is not to appear dull, so first of all, try out some ideas with coloured pencils on the paper pattern. To mix some delicate marble tints, take a brushful of clear paint and blend on the palette using only a drop of other colours, so that you are in control of the end result (see page 51). Remember to use the solvent and paper towels to clean the brush when changing colours.

6 Carefully apply the transparent glass paint, using the paintbrush, painting the design a section at a time. In this way the mount will look as though it were indeed made up of individual pieces.

7 This is a perfect opportunity to experiment with techniques. For a flat finish, generously paint, so that brush-marks disappear. Or for exciting marble and tortoiseshell effects, draw a brush with a little of a darker colour across the wet paint. Stippling the wet paint will give you a softly broken surface. The paints will dry in about ten minutes, and again a hair dryer will help, but allow two days for the paints to harden properly.

8 Replace the glass, taking care to avoid finger marks on painted areas. Reposition the mount and line it up carefully with the painted mount. Finally, lay the photograph in place and check again that all of the components are in line with each other, re-assembling into the frame.

Design directory

*This is a basic layout sheet for position-
ing designs on to a mirror. The patterns
supplied should be flipped from left to
right to cover each corner. You can
reduce or enlarge the designs to suit your
particular mirror.*

Colourful wine set

To explore colour combinations, see how dramatically one design can change, given three variations of colour treatment. Choose a traditional rose and emerald setting, rich magenta with turquoise and blue; or amber and ruby with mahogany.

The traditional lotus design reminiscent of the Art Nouveau movement is simplified here so that it will fit onto wine glasses. If your glasses are for everyday use, check that your paints will harden off sufficiently to withstand regular cleaning. This should take the form of a gentle wipe down with a damp, soapy cloth and then dry straight away. A straight-sided glass will be easier to start with. Remember that if your glass has a double curvature, like a goldfish bowl, it can be more difficult to position the design.

To overcome this problem, push crumpled newspaper into the glass behind the design to make it lie flat against the glass. In this way, the image is clear. You may well like to add a carafe to complete the set, but of course the design may not fit into the carafe you have chosen. In that case, you may be able to adjust the size on a photocopier or outline the design freehand.

TECHNIQUE FOCUS
Learning to combine colours
MATERIALS
Clear wine glasses
Your design
Outline paste
Transparent glass paints
Palette
The right solvent for the paints you have chosen
Basic equipment as listed on page 12

1 Clean the wine glasses well in hot, soapy water and then prepare your design. Position the design inside a glass, using a little masking tape to hold it in place and check that it fits neatly. Push crumpled newspaper in behind the design to make it lie flat against the glass.

2 Rest the glass in the masking tape reel to steady it and trace the design with the outline paste as far as you can reach round easily (see page 16). Mistakes can be wiped off with paper towels. Leave the outline paste for about ten minutes to dry naturally or use a hair dryer to speed it up. Once the outline is hard enough so that you will not damage it, turn the glass round and lay it in the tape reel with the blank side up, then complete the outline on this side.

3 Study the photographs on these pages and then decide on your choice of colours, or you could even create another colourway of your own to personalise this project.

4 Using the brush, paint the design with the transparent glass paints. Clean the brush when changing colours. Paint generously, so that the brush marks blend and flatten out. Excess paint can be wiped off the brush into the pot. It is better to put on too much paint than too little.

5 Finish each section on the wine glasses by brushing downwards over the paint, so that any runs that might have appeared will flatten themselves out. Leave the glass paint to harden off for at least a day, but preferably two, before using the glasses.

Design directory

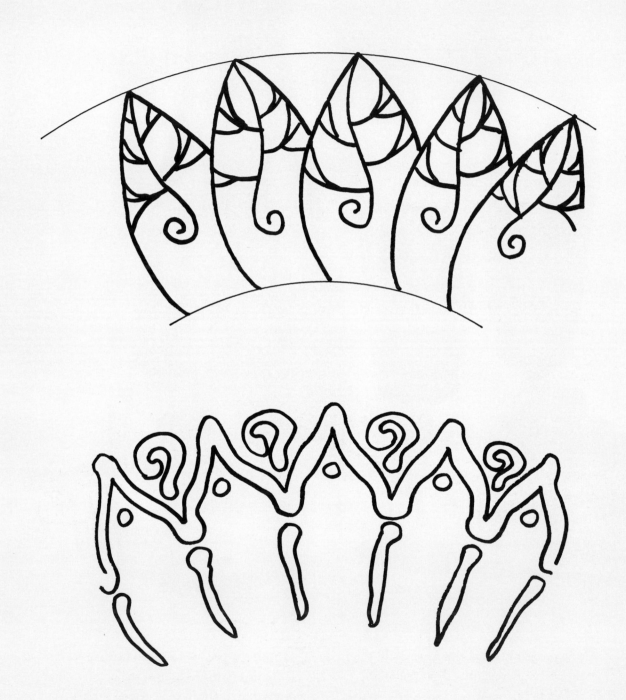

SPECIAL TECHNIQUES

This exciting stage in the build-up of your range of techniques brings us to variations and developments of every kind. Even the most simple method will bring your work to life with a professional touch. We consider outlines, thick and thin, silver and gold, etched glass, mirror glass, 'jewels', and wonderful rich paint finishes glowing with colour and texture.

Design directory

Etched glass candlesticks

Perfect for a special birthday, candlesticks always add a festive feel to any celebration. The designs are worked freehand, so have some fun working out your own pattern and experimenting with different colour schemes.

Just when you thought you had exhausted all the variations in glass, we come to etched glass and here this intriguing technique is carefully explored.

TECHNIQUE FOCUS
Painting on etched glass
MATERIALS
Etched glass wine bottles
Your design
Outline paste
Transparent glass paints
The right solvent for the paints you have chosen
Candles
Basic equipment as listed on page 12

1 For this project, the design cannot be traced because it is almost impossible to position it inside the glass bottles. So this is definitely one for freehand drawing. If you find the prospect of this daunting, try out the shapes first with pencil and paper until you are more confident.

2 Take great care to avoid handling the clean etched surface so hold the bottle by the top and bottom only. Draw on your design with the outline paste. Mistakes are more difficult to remove from an etched surface, so they are best disguised, if possible. Leave the outline paste for about ten minutes to dry naturally or use a hair dryer to speed up the drying time.

3 Paint only the areas you wish to become transparent, cleaning the brush with solvent and paper towels when changing colours. Like the outliner, paints will dry in about ten minutes, and again a hair dryer will help, but do allow two days to harden off properly.

4 Set the candle in place, shaving the base as necessary to make a good, steady fit. For an added finishing touch, you could tie a huge bow in your chosen colour scheme and add some dried flowers too.

This monochrome group of designs (right) shows some of the striking effects that can be achieved with surface textures and restrained use of colour. On the left, the pattern looks different in colour and monochrome.

Design directory

Mirror image

Add some sparkle to your life and decorate a plain mirror with this simple and richly-coloured scroll pattern repeat, learning some new and exciting techniques as you progress through the project.

The main difference between this project and the preceding ones is that the design has to be transferred to the mirror as it can't be traced. The method is described in detail at the beginning of this section (see page 73).

TECHNIQUE FOCUS

Painting on mirrors

MATERIALS

Square mirror tile (any size)

Your design

Carbon paper

Outline paste (gold)

Transparent glass paints

Palette (optional)

The right solvent for the paints you have chosen

Basic equipment as listed on page 12

1 Clean the mirror well. Prepare the design and enlarge or reduce it to the right size for your square mirror tile.

2 Position the design on the mirror tile, check that it fits well, and then transfer the design using carbon paper as described on page 73.

3 Follow the design in black outline paste making a thick line. To do this, move your hand much more slowly and squeeze the tube more firmly. It can be quite difficult to see the fine carbon line on the shiny surface. Make sure the light is good, and keep the design to hand so that you can check it. Mistakes can be wiped off with paper towels.

4 Paint over all the black outline (refer to pages 16–17), and experiment with any colours and ideas.

5 Leave to harden. Follow up with the thick gold line, moving your hand more slowly and squeezing a little harder. Make a few curls and spirals in the borders, or try some ideas on paper to practise first. Allow the pattern to harden for two days before you hang the mirror on the wall. You may choose to fix it directly to the wall with adhesive pads, or to a board painted in any of the popular decorative finishes.

Design directory

Decorative door panel

Here is a glorious garland with jewelled centres to bring a breath of summer sunshine to your front door all year round. The design would work equally well on a glass-fronted cupboard door or any window.

This project explores further the problems posed by a full-size project. The finished piece is held in place in the door with wooden battening. However, the exact profile of the wooden beading will depend upon your door, so you may need advice from a carpenter.

TECHNIQUE FOCUS

Using glass jewels

MATERIALS

Glass (to the size of your window)

Your design

Jewels

Fast-setting, two-part clear epoxy glue

Scrap of card

Toothpicks

Outline paste

Transparent glass paints

The right solvent for the paints you have chosen

Wooden beading

Saw

Hammer

Small nails

Basic equipment as listed on page 12

1 Use the paper towel to clean the glass, then prepare your design. You may need to make adjustments to the shape and size of the design, to fit your window. (This floral design is for a popular style of door.) Then place the design face up and position the glass on top of it. Tape it in place with masking tape.

2 Try the jewels in place over the design, and check for size. Select ones with the flattest base. Following the manufacturer's instructions, squeeze out a small blob of epoxy resin and next to it, a same size blob of epoxy hardener onto the cardboard. Use a toothpick to mix thoroughly.

3 Apply glue as directed to a jewel, and place in position on the glass, over the design. Hold the jewels in place with a small piece of masking tape as they tend to float and move off position. Repeat for all the flower centres and then leave the resin to harden. Fast-setting epoxy will usually start to harden in five minutes, so do only two or three jewels at a time.

4 Clean off any finger marks. Use the outline paste to trace the design. Run a line of paste around the base of each jewel where it meets the glass to conceal the glue line. Mistakes can be wiped off with paper towels. Leave the outline paste for about ten minutes to dry naturally or use a hair dryer to speed up the drying time. Remove the design from the back of the glass.

5 Paint generously, using the soft paintbrush with the transparent paints. Clean the brush with the solvent and paper towels when changing colours. Lift the glass off the table now and then to check that the colour is even. Like the outliner, paints will dry in about ten minutes, and again a hair dryer will help, but do allow two days for the paints to harden off properly.

6 To secure the glass in the door, measure and mitre the wooden batten. Place the painted flowers facing towards the existing window, leaving a small air-gap. Nail the mitred batten around the edge to secure it in place. To minimise condensation, place a tray of crystals within the air gap between the two pieces of glass, on advice from your glazier.

Design directory

Rose trinket boxes

These delightful trinket boxes feature iridescent glass nuggets which form a focal point to the design. The key to creating these boxes for a dressing table lies in a careful choice of colours and materials.

These plain boxes can be found in gift shops or look for something similar in second hand shops. They are perfect for transforming into exquisite dressing table ornaments. The design is a delicate tracery of gold outline paste, offset by the jewels and softly-coloured paints.

Any outline on the surface of the glass is vulnerable unless it is painted over, but we would not normally paint over gold. However, the soft rose and green paints allow the gold to shine through, giving a beautiful metallic finish.

MATERIALS

Brass and glass trinket box
Your design
Jewels
Fast-setting, two-part clear epoxy glue
Scrap of card
Toothpicks
Outline paste
Transparent glass paints
The right solvent for the paints you have chosen
Basic equipment as listed on page 12

1 Clean all the glass surfaces thoroughly, both the box and the jewel, with a damp, soapy cloth and then dry carefully.

2 Prepare your design and cut around it so that it will fit neatly inside the box. With the design facing up, secure it to the inside of the box lid with small pieces of masking tape. If the sides of the box are big enough, you can prepare and attach the side motifs in the same way. If the box is very small, consider drawing this simple pattern freehand.

3 Select a jewel with the flattest base and position it over the design and check for size. When you are satisfied that the jewel is right for the box, mix the epoxy resin according to the manufacturer's instructions. Use a toothpick to mix thoroughly and then apply to the jewel. Stick it in position on the lid. Hold the jewel in place with masking tape until the glue dries. Remove the tape once the glue has hardened.

4 Clean off any finger marks and outline the designs with the gold paste. Run a ring of paste around the base of the jewel to cover the join; mistakes can be wiped off with paper towels. Leave the outline paint to dry for about ten minutes or use a hairdryer to speed up the drying time. Remove the designs from inside the box.

5 Paint the box lid generously using the soft paintbrush with the transparent paints. Clean the brush with the solvent and paper towels when changing colour. Allow two days for the paints to harden off properly.

Bejewelled candlesticks

Enjoy the rich colours and encrusted surface texture of this candle-lit group. Many other items can be decorated in this way, such as the bowl and jar shown here. Pure self-indulgence – and why not?

For this project, the glass nuggets are used on three-dimensional surfaces which are not completely flat, so glue them firmly.

TECHNIQUE FOCUS

Encrusted surface using jewels and gold paste with glass paints

MATERIALS

Flat glass items
Your design
Glass jewels (rich colours)
Fast-setting, two-part clear epoxy glue
Scrap of card
Toothpicks
Outline paste (gold)
Transparent glass paints
The right solvent for the paints you have chosen
Basic equipment as listed on page 12

1 Select the jewels with the flattest bases, sort them for size and then make simple patterns, until you feel happy with the layout. Make notes or sketches of your final layout. Wash and dry all the items to clean them thoroughly, and then avoid handling them unnecessarily.

2 Rest your first glass item so that it is as steady and level as possible. Mix the epoxy resin according to the manufacturer's instructions. Using a toothpick, apply glue to the back of a jewel and position it on the glass, referring to your sketch layout. Hold the jewels in place with a small piece of masking tape as they tend to float and move off position. Leave the glue to harden. Repeat with each jewel to complete the design.

3 Carefully run a line of gold paste around the base of each jewel, where it meets the glass, to conceal the glue line. Leave the outline paste to dry and then finally paint the objects, as previously described.

4 Paint generously over the glass areas around the jewels, using the soft paintbrush with the transparent paints. Clean the brush with the solvent and paper towels when changing colours. Leave to dry.

5 Gold decorations of swirls and spirals add a finishing touch to the painted areas. Leave the piece to dry for two days.

This exuberant group of designs simply glitters with strong, dazzling colours to offer yet another rather exciting variation of surface textures on glass. These designs would be perfect in an exotic setting.

WORKING ON PLASTICS

Plastics are a new material for glass painters and, surprisingly, most paints will work on both glass and plastics. However, they will not work on all plastics, so test by applying the solvent used for your particular paint on a practice piece first. There are many different types of plastic, all with their own special properties, and the projects on the following pages offer you the opportunity to try a whole range of exciting decorative painting techniques.

TECHNIQUES FOR PLASTICS

So like glass superficially, plastics are particularly useful because they are lightweight and unbreakable. Obviously, this is most appealing if you are intending to glass paint with children. But plastics also have some unique characteristics.

Everyone knows how plastic attracts dust because of the static charge. Plastic is softer than glass, so greater care is needed in removing dust. Use a very soft cloth, working smoothly and slowly, to avoid creating a further charge.

More difficult to predict is the effect of the wide variety of glass paints, and their solvents, on the many different types of plastics. There is no universal answer, so simply try them out.

Take a drop of the right solvent for your paints on a brush, and paint a small area of the plastic that you hope to use. The worst that can happen is that the solvent will dissolve the plastic, or at least attack it. To avoid disappointment, try it out before starting your project.

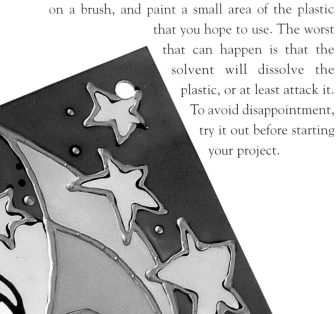

USING A FINE PEN ON FILM
Using a fine pen on film is exactly the same as for glass – see page 72. For information on choosing and testing the pen, also see page 72.

CHOOSING A GLUE
With plastic, you will need to check that the glue secures plastic film to wood, card and metal, without attacking the plastic. So test this out at the same time as the rest of the materials.

SEEING NEW ITEMS IN OLD PACKAGING
At the end of this section there are several projects that feature recycled pieces of packaging (see pages 114–119). While not strictly a glass painting technique, the effectiveness of a design will depend on just how suitable a piece of packaging is for the item in mind.

Those of you who have ever run projects for fund-raising, community events and children's groups, for example, will be overjoyed to see that you really can make something out of nothing.

SPECIAL TECHNIQUES FOR GLASS AND PLASTIC
The following techniques apply to both glass and plastics and will only be limited by the quality of your paints, so choose the best you can find.

PAINTING LARGE AREAS
A large area should be covered quickly, so that the paint flows and flattens itself out, without leaving brush marks. Take a brushful of paint at a time and sweep around the surface. If there is too much paint, you can easily spread it. Do not try to tidy it up at this stage; it is more important to keep the paint wet.

Once you have covered the whole surface, lift the design off the worksurface and check that there aren't any large gaps. If there are, fill them with a brushful of paint and blend into the areas around it. Lift the piece again for checking. Work quickly to smooth in any streaky areas, so that the glass paint does not dry messily.

Add more paint as needed. You can use the brush to lift off any excess paint and wipe it back into the pot. It is almost impossible to put on too much paint, though, because when the paint is really wet, it will smooth and flatten itself. And you will be surprised to find that although you seem to have put on a lot of glass paint, the level of the paint in the pot will not have changed noticeably.

WET ON DRY PAINTING

It is very difficult to give a second coat of paint, because it will dissolve the first coat. But details can be added very delicately to a first coat once it has hardened a little. For instance, veins could be added to leaves in a darker green. Or the rosy cheeks of the Sun (see below) were added as the golden yellow of the face was drying. Because of all the variables, experience is the best guide to the exact timing and result.

When a background has almost dried, reposition the design under the surface on which you are painting (it is not necessary to tape it in place this time). As you apply wet paint over the top, it will spread very slightly into the almost hardened paint.

WET ON WET PAINTING

Colours can be swirled about within each other or left side by side while the paint is wet to give a superb effect that is very like real stained glass. Sweep the colours with the brush or place drops of a second colour onto the first, where they will spread before your very eyes.

This process relies upon working very quickly, so to clean the brush, just squeeze it in the kitchen paper when changing colours. This works well, without contaminating the colours, because the paints are thick and do not leave a deposit in the jar.

Taking only one section at a time, apply paint in the relevant place. While it is still wet, squeeze the brush clean with a paper towel and paint the inner point of the same section with a second colour. Blend the wet colours gently together. Paint another section in the same way.

By this time, the first section will have started to dry so it is safe to add a third colour without it just spreading and dissolving into the first and second ones. Do not try to speed up this technique by drying the paint with a hair dryer, as forced drying will prevent the paint from flattening out.

Experience will tell you when the paint is exactly dry enough to achieve the desired effect, so take time to experiment. This technique produces a soft merging of colours with no defined edge.

The first coat of paint is left to dry completely before finishing touches are added to the stalks and centres of the flowers. This wet on dry technique gives definition to the edges of the colours.

Glittering squares

Let the kindly faces of the Sun and Moon light your way through more new techniques and materials. With each of these designs (on this page and overleaf), you are introduced to painting on a rigid plastic sheet.

The technique used for decorating the mirror project on pages 82–85 is repeated here on these iridescent lightcatchers However, in this case, the black outliner is used first, to separate the colours, as usual. Then, after the object has been painted, the gold or silver outline is used once again to add further decorations.

TECHNIQUE FOCUS

Painting on rigid plastic sheeting and using gold and silver outlines over a black outline

GOOD DAY SUNSHINE

There are more new paint techniques involved with this design; painting large areas, wet on wet (such as the cheeks and flames) to achieve a marbled effect, and wet on dry for the finer details.

MATERIALS

5 ¼in (35cm) square of rigid plastic sheet
Cutting tool
Felt-tipped pen
Flat piece of wood
Small clamp
Drill
Your design
Outline paste (black, gold)
Transparent glass paints
The right solvent for the paint you have chosen
Fine nylon thread
Gold parcel twine (optional)
Basic equipment as listed on page 12

1 Following the manufacturer's instructions, cut the plastic into a square of the desired size. Then use the felt-tipped pen to mark the position for the hanging hole – ½in (12mm) in from each side. Place the scrap of wood under the plastic square, at the position marked for the hole, and clamp both to the work surface. Drill the hole in the plastic square as marked, referring as necessary to the manufacturer's recommendations.

2 Wash the plastic with a soapy cloth and dry gently, taking care not to scratch it, as plastic is much softer than glass.

3 Prepare your design and then place it face up and position the plastic on top of it. Tape the design in place with masking tape.

4 Use the black outline paste to trace the design. Do not mark the dots on his cheeks (they are to be painted). Mistakes can be wiped off with paper towels. Leave the outline paste for about ten minutes to dry naturally or use a hair dryer to speed up the drying time. Remove the design from the back of the glass.

5 Start by painting the Sun's face, referring to the technique for painting large areas on page 96–97. Sweep yellow paint around the top edge of the face. Brush it out over the forehead and add another brushful of paint to that same area. Take another brushful of paint and spread it carefully below the eyes, blending in the

Squeeze the wet brush clean with a paper towel and paint the inner point of the same section with blue. Blend the wet colours gently together.

8 Paint another section in the same way. By this time, the first section will have started to dry, so it is safe to add the third colour without it just spreading and dissolving into the magenta and blue. Squeeze the brush clean in a paper towel, take a brushful of turquoise and add some drops of paint to the area where the magenta and blue paint blend together, in both of the sections painted so far.

9 Repeat the whole process, painting only two sections at a time, until you have finished all of the sky. Leave to dry for an hour.

10 The black outline served to separate the colours from each other. If gold had been used, it would have been lost beneath the paint. So now is the time to pipe the gold outline paste directly from the tube, as before, over the black outline, purely for decoration. Choose whether or not to include the Sun's features in gold, and follow the circle of the Sun's face and the sunrays. Add further decoration if desired. This will dry naturally in about ten minutes, but the process can be speeded up with a hair dryer. Allow the paint to harden off for two days.

paint from the forehead. Finally, take another brushful and sweep around the lower edge of his face. Spread it quickly and then add another brushful of paint to that area. To tidy up the surface, see page 96. Allow the face to dry slightly. Paint the wavy sunrays in yellow, too.

6 The next step requires a wet on dry painting technique (see page 97). Reposition the design under the plastic square. Then make an orange colour on the palette by mixing together yellow and a little red. Paint drops of orange onto the dots marked on the pattern for his cheeks. Allow it to spread into the slightly wet paint. Use orange to paint the straight sunrays and his mouth. Use the solvent and paper towels to clean the brush thoroughly.

7 To paint the rest of the sun, use the wet on wet technique described on page 97. Taking only one section at a time, paint the outer edge of a sky section with magenta.

11 Tie some of the nylon thread through the hole and hang from a hook at your window. Golden parcel twine would add a decorative finishing touch.

OVER THE MOON

This complementary design is just as simply made, but uses silver outline paste for the decorative details.

MATERIALS

5 ¼in (35cm) square of rigid plastic sheet
Cutting tool
Felt-tipped pen
Flat piece of wood
Small clamp
Drill
Your design
Outline paste (black, silver)
Transparent glass paints
The right solvent for the paint you have chosen
Fine nylon thread
Silver parcel twine (optional)
Basic equipment as listed on page 12

1 Follow Steps 1 to 4 for the Sun. For painting the Moon, start by painting the blue sky to the left of the moon, covering it quickly as in Step 4 of the Sun. After covering all of the sky with blue paint, brush inwards to blend around the stars. Add another brushful of paint to that area. Now is the time to tidy it all up. Lift it off the work surface and neaten as for the Sun.

2 Paint the right-hand side of the design in magenta, using the same method as above. Plan your route, beginning at the top corner and painting around the stars. Then fill in the right-hand corner and paint around the stars and finally, the lower corner, and paint around the stars. At each stage, blend the paint over the large areas, and then add a further brushful of paint and spread it out. Then lift the plastic square off the work surface and check for uneven patches.

3 Smooth and blend all areas, adding more paint as necessary, or wiping off excess with

the brush. Use the solvent and paper towels to clean the brush. Allow the painted area to dry naturally. Paint the left-hand side of the moon's face in yellow.

4 For the moon, blend clear paint on the palette with a very little white paint. Then paint the translucent white on the upper and lower tips of the crescent moon. Lift the square off the work surface, and hold it over a dark background so that uneven patches will show. Smooth and blend the paint, adding more if necessary, and then leave to flatten out. Clean the brush.

5 For the right-hand side of the face, blend a little yellow paint with the translucent white on the palette. After painting, lift the square off the work surface, and hold it over a dark background, so that uneven patches will show. Smooth and blend the paint, adding more if necessary, and then leave to flatten out. Clean the brush well with solvent and a paper towel. There should be no residue of white left on the brush.

6 Use the wet on wet technique (see page 97) to finish off the Moon. Mix yellow and a little red to blend orange on the palette, and paint his mouth orange. Use the solvent and paper towels to clean the brush thoroughly. Leave to dry for an hour. Finish off the Moon with silver outline paste, as for the gold of the Sun described in Step 10.

7 Tie a thin thread through the hole and hang from a hook, at your window. Silver twine would add a finishing touch.

Design directory

Stained glass cards

A hand-crafted card is a pleasure to give and to receive. Glass painting techniques can be used on the plastic film window for beautiful stained glass greetings cards that will bring lasting memories to friends and loved ones.

Here are some ideas to delight your favourite children on their birthdays – the clear, bright primary colours will be a great success. The Design Directory gives further motifs for making cards for all occasions; birthdays, Christmas, good luck, moving home and many more. For information about lightweight plastic film, see page 96.

TECHNIQUE FOCUS
Painting on plastic film

MATERIALS
Large, three-fold greetings card with
a central aperture
Thin plastic film
Glue suitable for paper and plastic
Your design
Outline paste
Transparent glass paints
The right solvent for the paint you have chosen
Basic equipment as listed on page 12

1 Trim the plastic film so that it is just slightly smaller than the section of the card with the aperture. Lightly clean off any finger marks and dust to avoid scratching the film.

2 Now use masking tape to secure your 'window' very lightly over the central aperture of the card, and trace all the way around it with the outline paste to indicate the outside edge of the design. Then carefully remove the 'window' from the card.

3 Prepare your design, then place it face up and position the film on top of it, making sure to line up the frame with the picture. Tape the design in place with masking tape.

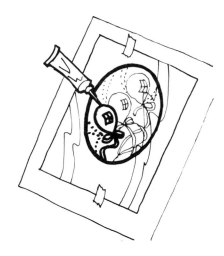

4 Use the outline paste to trace the design. Mistakes can be wiped off with paper towels. Leave the outline paste for about ten minutes to dry naturally. Then carefully remove the design from the back of the film.

5 Use the small, soft brush to paint generously, just as for painting on glass – lift the film off the table now and then to check the paint is even. Clean the brush with the solvent and paper towels when changing colours.

6 Test the glue first to check that it really works with both the film and the card, and does not attack the film. Open out the card and lay it flat, face down. Rub the glue all around the

aperture and also along the top and bottom edges of the card. Lay the painted window face down lightly over the aperture. Lift carefully and check that the frame is in line with the aperture. Adjust the film if necessary, and then rub down gently into place.

7 Do not glue down the two outer leaves of the card. When it stands, the light can shine through, bringing the iridescent colours to life. Allow the paints to harden off throughly for at least two days before finally slipping the card into the envelope.

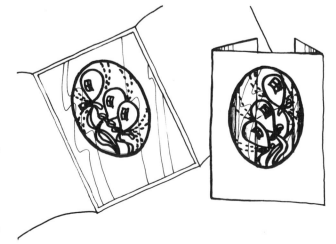

Design directory

Doll's house windows

Escape into a whole world of delight! The care and patience needed to paint these windows will not tax those who love doll's houses and miniatures, and the results are so rewarding for the true enthusiast.

Doll's house enthusiasts will be acquainted with the wonderful conservatory and garden settings which are now available. They offer endless scope for colour and design and in the Design Directory on pages 112–113 you can find a design of fuchsias for a conservatory, and a wisteria for a greenhouse.

All the designs and details are to the standard $\frac{1}{12}$in scale. Most dolls' houses already have windows of plastic sheeting in place. You will need to decide whether or not to decorate the actual windows directly, or to paint on film and 'double glaze' your doll's house, exactly as you would for a full-sized window for your own home.

Instructions are given here for the double glazing method. It is easier to position the windows for painting, and less of a worry if you make a mistake.

TECHNIQUE FOCUS
Drawing with pen and ink on film

MATERIALS
Tracing or greaseproof paper, or thin card
Your design
Waterproof pen
Small piece of plastic film
Small, sharp scissors
Transparent glass paints
The right solvent for the paint you have chosen
Glue for plastic, metal, wood and card
Basic equipment as listed on page 12

1 Make a template of the windows using the paper or thin card. Trace the design onto the tracing or greaseproof paper. Compare it with your template. You may need to add a repeat of the design, or decide on a part to leave out. Make a clear drawing of the amended design.

2 With the waterproof pen, draw around your template onto the film, to indicate the shape and size of the window. Use the scissors to trim the film to a size large enough to handle, with room for tape at the edges. Then with a piece of paper towel, remove any finger marks from the film slowly to avoid attracting further dust. Place the design face up and position the film on top of it. Tape it in place with masking tape.

3 Use the pen to trace the design. The ink will usually dry naturally, within about five minutes. Remove the design from the film.

4 Paint the film carefully with the glass paints, cleaning the brush with the solvent and paper towels when changing colours. Carefully lift the film off the table now and then to check that the colour is even. The paints will dry in about ten minutes.

5 Trim the window to size with the scissors, taking great care not to leave finger marks on the painted surface. Finally, glue the window in place in your doll's house.

Design directory

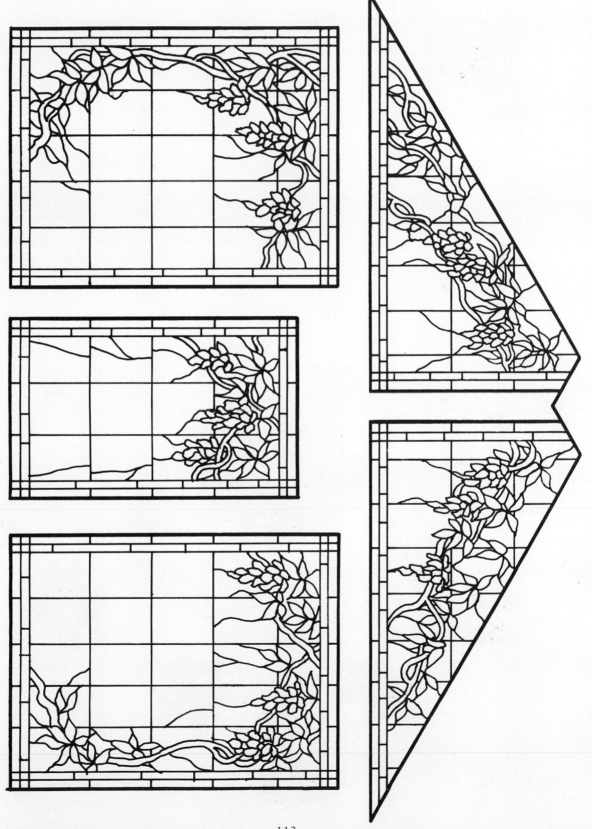

Too pretty to throw away

We all notice how attractive some packaging is, and many of us, reluctant to throw it out, hoard bits and pieces, in the certain knowledge that we will eventually find a use for it all. Well, you were right!

Plastics vary widely, from brittle to squashy, and so behave differently. Before you start, take a little of the solvent for your paints on a brush and check that it does not attack the plastic.

TECHNIQUE FOCUS
Seeing new items in old packaging

LIGHT AS AIR

What could be prettier than the delicate shapes of a coloured mobile fluttering and spinning gently with each breath of air? Hung by an open garden window or above a baby's cot, it adds all the charm and movement of a butterfly.

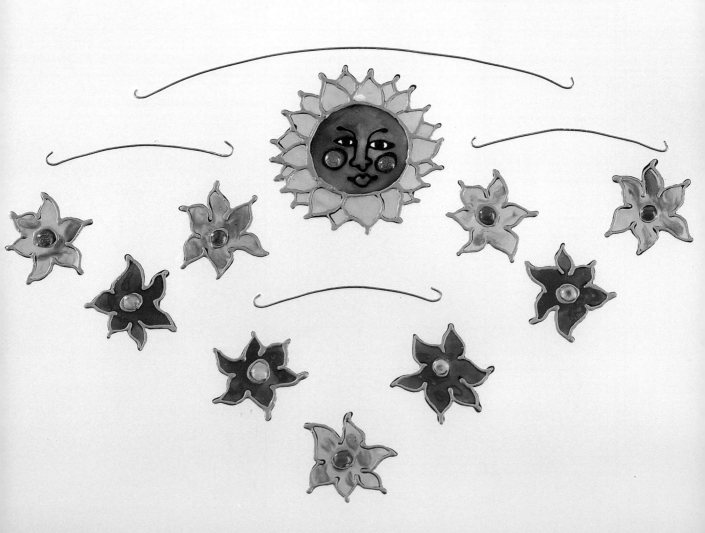

MATERIALS

Your design

Plastic film from packaging

Outline paste

Transparent glass paints

The right solvent for the paint you have chosen

Sewing needle (medium-sized)

Small, sharp scissors

Cotton or nylon thread

Thin wire

Decorative ribbon (optional)

Basic equipment as listed on page 12

1 It is easier to handle one large sheet of film than several tiny pieces, so cut out the finished pieces at the end. Clean the film lightly so that further dust won't be attracted to it. Then prepare your design, place it face up and position the plastic sheet on top. Tape in place with masking tape.

2 Use the outline paste to trace the design. Mistakes can be wiped off with paper towels. Leave the outline paste for about ten minutes to dry naturally. Remove the design.

3 Paint generously, using the soft paintbrush with the transparent paints. Clean the brush with the solvent and paper towels when changing colours. Lift the plastic off the table now and then to check that the colour is even. Like the outliner, paints will dry in about ten minutes.

4 You may like to add the outline to the other side of the piece too, so that the backs are finished to the same standard. Allow to dry.

5 It is easier to make the hole for hanging first of all. Use the needle to pierce a neat hole, and then, with the scissors, cut out the shapes. Tie on a length of thread and follow the photograph to assemble your mobile. A ribbon bow makes a pretty finishing touch.

VARIATIONS

How about making some really unusual gift tags from recycled plastic in exactly the same way? Remember to cut out the tags only after you have painted the plastic and left it to dry. It makes handling the plastic so much easier. Make a set of matching decorations to hang on a Christmas tree, or perhaps a little light-weight roundel for the window. Try a sparkly variation with gold or silver paste, and sprinkle glitter into the paste before it dries. Or add a sequin or two, and hang with a glittery gift-wrap thread.

SHELL-LIKE EARRINGS

Make these beautiful shell-like earrings in exactly the same way as for the mobile, but after cutting out the finished pieces of painted film, hang on earring loops instead of making into a mobile. Light as a feather, with a wide choice of designs, these pieces will make delightful presents to please all your friends – and all for next to nothing.

Design directory

Bathroom collection

Large gift packaging often makes an appearance following a special celebration. These lovely jars appeared after one Christmas and as soon as I saw them, I knew they would be ideal for storing jewel-coloured bath pearls and oils.

The sides of the jars suggested that they would be perfect for panels of fish and shell motifs in contrasting colourways, which were then outlined with black paste for definition.

TECHNIQUE FOCUS
Recycling large polythene containers

MATERIALS
Large, plastic jar with a screw-on lid
Your design
Outline paste
Transparent glass paints
Palette
The right solvent for the paint you have chosen
Basic equipment as listed on page 12

1 Peel off the labels and wipe away any traces of adhesive. Many different adhesives are used for labels, so finding out what will work best has to be through trial and error. Try soap and water first. Then, with the brush, test a drop of the solvent for your paints to see if it attacks the plastic.

2 Prepare your designs and then trim them to size so that they will fit inside the jars. Use a little masking tape to position them inside the jars, facing outwards.

3 Clean off any finger marks with a piece of paper towel. Then use the outline paste to trace the designs. Black outline paste has been used here, but you could consider using either silver or gold, if you preferred. Mistakes can be wiped off with paper towels. Leave the outline paste for about ten minutes. Remove the designs from the back of the plastic and reposition them facing outwards, on the other side. When the paste on the first side is hard enough, trace the motif onto the other side of the jar. Leave to dry as before and repeat, as desired.

4 Paint generously, cleaning the brush with the solvent and paper towels when changing colours. Consider using your palette to mix a drop of white into all of the colours so that they will show up against the dark background. Look out for any places where the paint may form a run, and lightly brush it downwards. The paints will dry in about ten minutes, but do allow at least two days to harden off properly, as this item will be handled constantly.

5 To clean subsequently, wash only with a soft, soapy cloth and dry at once. Never soak. A ribbon in a contrasting shade of colour makes a pretty finishing touch.

JEWELLERY BOX
Who would ever guess that this charming little jewellery box was originally a birthday gift that contained a selection of delicious chocolates? Everyone I know has kept one or more of these boxes because they are simply 'too pretty to throw away'. With only a little decoration they take on a new lease of life. Follow the same methods as described for the bathroom jars.

Design directory

Trouble shooting

Occasionally, things will go wrong when you are painting, so here is a helpful checklist of potential problems with their solutions.

GLASS

A decorative front door panel, or any large project, will be quite heavy, so do not try to hang it on the glass. It should not swing freely on any door, such as a patio door, which is in constant use. A glass panel added to any existing door or window should be fixed firmly, using either a wooden beading or a secondary double glazing system to support it completely. You may need to consider asking advice about crystals to minimise condensation, too.

LEAD

Uneven lead edging on a roundel can be avoided by pinching the lead at closer intervals as you roll it. Wider gaps between pinching can allow a sharper upstand to develop, which may form a crease when burnished. Squash these sharp upstands down against the glass before burnishing.

A one-sided lead edge, which has crept off-centre, may not be noticeable once the design is painted. If the lead will support the eyelet for hanging, it is not a problem. If it is not going to support it, the lead must come off! Check as you roll that the lead is centred, and remember that you are not committed until you have burnished the lead down.

OUTLINER

A blocked tube makes such a mess if it bursts. It will wash out with water if treated at once but this can be avoided by these simple precautions.

Always keep paper towels to hand. When you first feel that the paste is not flowing easily, look at the nozzle. With a long pin, check that the nozzle is clear, and then run some water through it. If the nozzle was blocked, it may be simply because the top had not been replaced after use, so that will sort it out.

If it happens repeatedly, it is possible that the paste itself has at some time been stored in poor conditions, where frost could attack it. You should discuss this with your supplier.

Surprisingly, another cause of the burst tube is simply that it was never sufficiently open to allow the paste out! It is always a good idea to squeeze from the rolled end too, because the tube is less likely to burst.

A blobby outline can be annoying, so remember to wipe the nozzle on a paper towel before starting. Check that there is no air trapped in the tube by squeezing the tube slowly into the towel. You will feel it pop if that is the case, and then it should be fine to use.

If it continues to ooze, have you pressed too hard or is the tube dented? You can rectify this by squeezing the sides of the tube at the bottom, to suck the paste back in. Adjust your pressure to achieve the quality of line you want.

The outliner will also be affected by extremes of weather conditions, which can make the paste ooze out, harden in the nozzle or spread on contact with the glass. You will also find that each different make of paste handles differently.

A thick outline may worry you. Do remember that real stained glass is supported by the characteristic network of lead, so thick black lines are very much a part of this craft. You will find that your eye takes in the colour rather than the line once it is painted, so be prepared to experiment.

Perhaps your outline paste is simply too thick for the chosen design. It may work if you just simplify the design, or make it larger.

You could also invest in an engineering pen, as described on page 8, to give you a delicate quality of line.

Mistakes and smudged outlines can be wiped off with a paper towel while still wet. The neatest method is to dry it with a hair dryer on a medium setting, and to scrape off just that bit. Then restore the outline with paste again.

PAINTS

A streaky finish is usually due to applying too little paint. (See Painting Large Areas on page 96.) Unfortunately, some poor quality paints are thin and never give a good colour and even finish.

A second coat of paint should be avoided if possible, because it will break up the first coat. It may be advisable to scrape off the first coat and start again. If a second coat is really necessary, it can be applied after the first has hardened properly, but keep it light and quick, and then leave it. Remember that you could paint on both sides of the glass if it helps. One good generous coat of a quality paint is much better, if possible.

Paint on the lead edge can be wiped off as you go, with a corner of a paper towel, without disturbing the paint on the picture. If the paint is dry, moisten a soft cloth with a little of the solvent and slowly wipe the paint until it dissolves. To avoid the problem, run the paintbrush along the side of the lead edge in several long, sweeping strokes.

Paint in the wrong place is easily lifted off with your brush while it is still wet. Dry the brush with a tissue and pick up the paint with the dry brush, repeating as necessary. If the paint has dried, it can be scraped off with a craft knife. Then clean the glass carefully with a little solvent on the brush to dissolve the bit that went wrong. Wipe the brush on a tissue, and repeat until it has gone.

DESIGNS

Adjusting the size may lead to problems with line thickness (see thick outlines on page 122). You may need to make a further drawing of the design using tracing paper and a felt-tipped pen of the same thickness as the outline paste. If the design has been reduced, it may have become too complicated for this line thickness, and will need to be simplified. It is better to find that out beforehand when you can do something about it.

GLOBAL SPHERE SHAPES

These present a different problem when you want to trace a design because of the double curvature. You will need to take 'tucks' in the design, so take care that you do not lose too much of the design.

CLEANING

Lanterns and jars used around the home are quite likely to need regular cleaning, so here are some guidelines for you to follow.

Paints vary so much that you will need to carry out your own test on a sample. Some hobby paints will not survive under a hot tap, for example, or do not like being soaked.

They have a better chance if you have given them at least two weeks to harden off, so that the solvents have really had the time to evaporate and you have a good, lacquered finish. Make sure that you have painted over all the outline to protect it.

Once they have hardened off, quality paints can be washed under hand-hot water, with a wipe of washing-up liquid on a soft cloth, a rinse and dry, but again, avoid soaking.

WORKING IN GROUPS

Because jars are readily available, I am often asked how groups such as youth clubs, day-care centres and schools can best set this up as a fund raising project. The simplest way is to find a plug-socket, push a table up against it, and plug in a hair dryer. This saves so much drying time.

Work in groups of no more than four at a time. The paste and paints will usually go a long way, so if each person has his or her own outline paste, the paints can be shared. Each pot should have its own brush, so that the paints stay clean. Provide paper towels to accompany each brush. Solvent based paints cannot be poured out into a shallow palette, like powder paints, because the smell would empty the place in minutes! I make my paints topple-proof by filling a low sandwich box with sawn-off tubes from kitchen rolls. This is a good place for the solvent, too, for cleaning brushes and spills.

ESSENTIALS

Remember the paper towels and make sure you cover everything with newspapers. Encourage good working habits: always replace tops as you go – it saves paste hardening in the nozzle, or else oozing out. It also keeps the smell down, stops evaporation, and makes spills less likely. Worth the effort.

CARE OF NIGHTLIGHTS

Not all nightlights are suitable for use in a high-sided container, so read the manufacturer's notes when you buy. I lower the lighted candle into the jar using a pair of scissors like tongs. If you put the candle in first, you can burn yourself trying to light it, and a taper is not too good, because the flame burns up the taper, being at the wrong angle to catch the wick. You may come up with other ideas, but I have never had any problems.

The glass does get warm, but not too hot, because there is plenty of room for the heat to escape. All the same, ensure that an adult is always in the same room as any lighted candles. I also keep a tin lid at hand as an extinguisher.

TRANSPORTING A FINISHED PIECE

Great caution is needed here. The longer a piece is allowed to harden before being moved, the better. Handle a roundel only by its edges, and bunch up your fingers into the top of a jar. Do not think of bubble wrap, which may seem like the obvious answer: it will only print bubbles all over the paint.

It is probably best to rest your finished piece in the bottom of a box. It should never, for instance, be placed face downwards on the car seat, nor in a polythene bag. A roundel can travel well face upwards on a blanket, but take care that it will not slide about as you go around a corner.

EXTREMES OF TEMPERATURE

The outline paste suffers most from extremes of heat or cold, so never leave it in a car overnight. Always protect it from frost and from condensation which will form on the cold glass, particularly if the paint is still fresh, or if you have only done the outline. You will find that condensation will soak under the outline, lifting it so that you can slide it all over the place. You will then have to scrape it all off and start again.

WHERE TO GO FROM HERE

Develop your own designs. Any strong clear drawing will work, so make a drawing from a calendar or greetings card. Or is someone in the family a railway enthusiast? Has a friend just had a baby? You can make a roundel specially for them. Look at children's colouring books too for inspiration.

If you are selling any quantity for profit, even for fund raising, think about copyright. Stick to universal emblems like the fleur de lys, a local crest or traditional hearts and flowers. Or do you prefer the 'real thing'? If so, look at books on stained glass, make drawings of local doors, or take photographs.

Then take a small section of the design, or reduce the whole thing on a photocopier. Whatever your taste and style, take care not to make it too small and complicated for the paste to cope with.

Useful Addresses

UK

GLASS PAINTS
Dunsterville Craft & Design
48 Coningsby Road
High Wycombe
Buckinghamshire
HP13 5NY
(Mail order and craft shows
Paints, lead, designs, projects,
all English manufacture)

Heathcraft
1st floor balcony
22 Byram Arcade
Westgate
Huddersfield
West Yorkshire
HD1 1ND
(General craft supplies includ-
ing glass paints by Marabu,
Deka and Pebeo)

Deka Atlas Craft
4 Plumtree Street
The Lace Market
Nottingham
N61 1JL

Philip & Tracey Ltd
North Way
Andover
Hampshire
SP10 5BA
(Pebeo glass paints and Cerne
outliner)

Do It All
Branches throughout the UK
(Decra-Led for paints and
adhesive lead products)

Dryad Handicrafts
PO Box 38
Northgates
Leicester
LE1 9BU
(Glass painting workstation
from leading stationers)

DOLL'S HOUSE
CONSERVATORIES AND
GREENHOUSES
Lance and Jo Kerridge
129 Boundary Road
Wooburn Green
High Wycombe
Buckinghamshire

PAPERWEIGHTS
H Thorn & Son
118–119 Fore Street
Exeter
Devon

GLASS BLANKS
The Glass Studio
Sunshine Farm Crafts
Hilton
Lane Essington
Wolverhampton
WV1 2AU

GREETINGS CARDS
Craft Creations Ltd
Units 1–7
Harpers Yard
Ruskin Road
Tottenham
London
N17 8QA

STAINED GLASS SUPPLIES
Tempsford Stained Glass
Tempsford
Nr Sandy
Bedfordshire
SG19 2A
(for those who are inspired to
try the real thing)

James Hetley & Co Ltd
Glass House Fields
London
E1 95A

US

Plaid
QVC shopping channel on
cable and satellite TV
(glass paints)

Acknowledgments

A big thank you to the many friends who have helped in so many ways with testing products, trying out ideas and keeping supplies rolling for the mail order and craft shows. The list includes Nuala Brown, Sarah Jordan, Maggie Bedford, Brian Cook and Ted, Jean Colbear, Mandy Stenning, Chris Carter, Lorretta Halling and Cathy Hopkins, and all the lovely enthusiastic craftworkers at my classes and the craft shows. But chiefly, thanks to my dear husband John, who kept the pages turning.

Index